How To Wash A Heart

How To
Wash A Heart

Bhanu Kapil

First published 2020 by
Liverpool University Press
4 Cambridge Street
Liverpool
L69 7ZU

British Library Cataloguing-in-Publication data
A British Library CIP record is available

ISBN 978-1-789-62168-6 softback

Typeset by Carnegie Book Production, Lancaster
Printed and bound by CPI Group (UK) Ltd, Croydon CR0 4YY

Like this?

It's inky-early outside and I'm wearing my knitted scarf, like
John Betjeman, poet of the British past.

I like to go outside straight away and stand in the brisk air.

Yesterday, you vanished into those snowflakes like the ragged beast
You are.

Perhaps I can write here again.

A "fleeting sense of possibility." – K.

Keywords: Hospitality, stars, jasmine,
Privacy.

You made a space for me in your home, for my books and clothes,
and I'll

Never forget that.

When your adopted daughter, an "Asian refugee"

As you described her,

Came in with her coffee and perched on the end

Of my cot, I felt so happy.

And less like a hoax.

Showed her how to drink water

From the bowls

On the windowsill.

I don't want to beautify our collective trauma.
Your sexual brilliance resided, I sometimes thought,
In your ability to say,
No matter the external circumstances:
"I am here."
From this place, you gave only this many
Desiccated fucks
About the future.
Day by day, you discovered what happiness is.
As your guest, I trained myself
To beautify
Our collective trauma.
When night fell at last, I turned with a sigh
Towards the darkness.
I am about to squeeze out an egg, you
Murmured
As you kissed me
Goodnight.
Hold a funeral for the imagination,
I thought.

To my left is a turquoise door and to my right, a butcher's
Table.
Above you is a heart
Beating in the snow.
When I described the set of my play, an environment
More vivid to me
Than the memory
Of my childhood home, your
Face
Turned green.
What made you know something was over?
The milk in your eyes
Scared me.
In that moment, I understood that you were a wolf
Capable of devouring
My internal organs
If I exposed them to view.
Sure enough, the image of a heart
Carved from the body
Appeared
In the next poem you wrote.

There's a bright caul of fire
And cream
As I write these words, stretching out
These early spring or late winter
Mornings with coffee
And TV.
I don't remember
The underneath,
Everything I will miss when I die.
It's exhausting to be a guest
In somebody else's house
Forever.
Even though the host invites
The guest to say
Whatever it is they want to say,
The guest knows that host logic
Is variable.
Prick me.
And I will cut off the energy
To your life.

How to wash a heart:
Remove it.
Animal or ice?
The curator's question reveals
Their power style.
If power implies relationship,
Then here we are
At the part where even if something
Goes wrong,
That's exactly how it's meant to be.
Your job is to understand
What the feedback is.
It's such a pleasure to spend time
Outside the house.
There's nowhere to go with this
Except begin:
To plunge my forearms
Into the red ice
That is already melting
In the box.

My spiritual power was quickly depleted
By living with you.
Like an intrusive mother, you
Cared for my needs
But also, I never knew
When you might open my door, leaving it open
When you left.
My identity as a writer was precarious
During the time
I lived with you.
Once, you locked me in.
An accident.
My spine against a tree
When I dreamed that night.
Contact nature
On all fours, said the counselor,
Slipping off her chair onto the floor.
Help me to repair
What is broken and immortal.
Is that the bin?

I come from a country
All lime-pink on the soggy map.
Destroy me,
My soul whispered.
Eat me, bones and all.
Crush me in a vise.
Stop me
From walking out
That door.
The balloon deity
I made from the condom
On the floor
Was purgative, revolting,
Brilliant.
Her lips were pursed.
It doesn't matter
That you made so many mistakes,
She said.
Violence rots the brain.
Go.

I do not enjoy eating too much.
It's so painful.
The only remedy is the bitter herb
That grows by a rushing brook.
Oils, sugars, pearls, crushed diamonds, linens and songs
Populate your crappy cabinets.
Make a list of what you need
And I will get it, you ungrateful cow.
This is what I need:
The light and the heat and the yesterday
Of my work.
A candle on the wonky table at dusk.
How thyme migrates.
The chalky blue flowers.
I need something that burns as slowly
As that.
Because living with someone who is in pain
Requires you to move in a different way.
You bang the cup down
By my sleepy head.

Don't forget me, I whisper to my
Father.
Give me something to eat, I'm
So hungry, I call out to my
Mother.
The conditional care
Of even these
Imaginary parents
Excretes a hormonal load.
Am I safe with you?
Or like a baby crawling on the bumpy
Carpet, am I my own
Mother, actually?
Imagine a baby developing so rapidly
That by nightfall
It has ripped through the pale blue
Smock to evolve
Beyond the limits of the human.
I remember
How my mother woke me up
So early
To look at the bloody stars.

My grandfather fermented the yoghurt
With rose petals
And sugar then buried it
In the roots of a mango tree.
Come here, he said, extending
The sweetest fruit I have ever tasted
Come June.
On the far side of the orchard
He grew saffron and the mangoes there
Were red and pink.
In the dry well
He planted a pomegranate tree.
This is where they threw
The bodies
Come August
Noon.
Can you find your way home
By smell?
Metallic, the air tilts along a diagonal line.
I smell the pollen of the flowers of the mango tree
Which once concealed
A kill.

For lunch, my mother made okra
With caramelized onions,
A feat! The wet caps
She stuck to my forehead, cheeks
And nose.
Grimacing as the gates of the school
Swung open, I was
A joke.
The children who were children
Like me
Fled.
I was alone with the slime
Dripping down the neck
Of my red and white dress,
Nettle bites lucid on my shins.
Because I ran through the alleyways
And not the streets
To get here:
A hot yard.
Shame invites the sun
To live in the anus, the creases
Of the throat.

The priest brought my mother home.
My father fell over in the snow
After drinking his guts out.
The world
Was falling down around my ears.
When our neighbors
Said go, we fled,
Our hearts beating
Like a fish.
Hello, sang Lionel Richie, on the taxi's orange
Radio.
My grandfather burned his notebooks
Then scraped the ash
Into a hole
He could button up.
Don't ask me to remember
The word for zip.
My secret is this:
Though we lost all our possessions,
I felt
A strange relief
To see my home explode in the rearview mirror.

Monoracial, we fetched up
In a place without
Discrete racial categories.
Our hair
No longer felt like our hair
No matter how long
We combed it
With milk.
The messages we received
Were as follows:
You are a sexual object, I have a right
To sexualize you.
You are not an individual.
You are here
For my entertainment.
You complain too much.
Your sexual identity is not
Important.
The way you talk about what happened to you
Is a catastrophic representation.
Merry Christmas,
Little pig.

"A scream was heard.
A scream."
Psychosis creams the air
Giving it a peculiar richness
And depth.
I dissolve a lozenge
Beneath my tongue
For courage.
But now Will Ransome
And Cora Seaborne
Have fallen in love
And I feel so much better.
Peel an orange
From the market.
Remove it from a paper bag.
The city like a thin piece of muslin
Stretched over the drain-pipes,
Steeples
And bees.
A grey ribbon tied around the wrist.
You could see it growing taut.
Please.

Here in the black and silver café now and
It's wonderful.
I love the alien foliage
In the bathroom.
D. is reading *Madame Bovary*
In a translation
By Lydia Davis.
My first friend in this country
Is gorgeous,
Lanky and blonde.
How long have I been
Gone?
I rarely think of the bright brown eyes
Of my childhood friends,
The unreachable memories
Of foraging
For red and white toadstools
In the forest.
Though the outer conditions
Are xenophobic,
I only want
To bask in this exotic friendship.

I was born feet-first beneath a Lebanon cedar
At 10.23 a.m.
On a November morning
So long ago
That many people who were alive that day,
Flinching from a sudden rain,
No longer walk upon this earth.
I am going to take you by surprise.
I am going to make you
So proud of me.
When you watch my plays, your heart
Will make a circuit with the dense shadow
In the upper part of the atmosphere.
The clouds
Will rain green frogs
The size of fingernails
And we will scoop them up
With our hands.
Sometimes I lie on the earth face down
To connect
With its copper plate.
You won't have to love me
For very long.

Tell me about your long journey,
You said, that
First day. Are your children
White?
I was confused by the question.
Perhaps I misheard.
What was it
Like?
I said: "There was a river and the poets
Loved to soar in its pellid
Current, a goat
Deprived of its innards, then sealed,
Inflated, sewn up by a cobbler
In a nearby colony.
When the snakes appeared
For the first time, the poets
Sat on the banks of the river
With a hand-stitched flag and sang
A song called *Gugga*."
No, you said.
I want to hear what happened afterwards
Not before.

On the second day, your daughter,
Adopted at the age
Of ten, appeared
At the brim of my bed.
I was still healing, unable
To re-set.
"It's not the men who exile me,
It's the women. I don't trust
The women," wrote
Aurora Levins Morales.
It was already clear to me
That you would
Dig up the sky, but this,
Your daughter's visit,
I could
Tolerate.
When's the last time you saw
A werewolf?
It's extraordinary how afraid I am
All the time.
What I would have said.
Speak.

On the third day, you invited
Half your neighborhood
To glimpse the red leaf
You had placed
Like a thing of beauty
In the pudding basin
Of tap water by the door.
Was I your art?
My involvement with your family
Was an act of volition
And consensus.
The political face you showed
To your neighbors,
For example, was contra-
Regime.
My links to the community
Of writers I had been a part of
Had broken overnight.
And so, I smiled
And laughed when you did.
I was not stupid.
I was not confused.

On the fourth day, I dreamed
Of early scenes.
How villagers cooked bread
With sugar then threw it
In the river. The fish
Gobbled it up.
Sure enough, the drought
Ended.
Once, they burned my dolls
And all the hand-made dolls
Of the girls in the village.
What will you sacrifice
For rain?
Imagine a heart
Suspended
In the moody-blue sky
Above the pyramid
Of orange clay.
With a bright voice, a voice
That was too loud,
You broke my trance.
Is she really still asleep?

On the fifth day, my cousin
Barged in.
He was an architect of pre-war
Life.
In the oily bag he offered me,
Deep-fried savory pastries
Gleamed.
Do you remember when Bumma
Ran into the trees
And roared like a lion,
Reciting his poetry from the bushes?
Binna was so jealous,
Whispering to the listeners: "ISN'T IT BORING?"
Do you remember
How insulted Bumma was?
"I hope the lions eat you
Next time," he shouted, stomping off!
Yes,
I remember.
Like thunder and meteors,
Your visit reminds me
Who I really am.

On the sixth day, I broke
A vase. You
Went crazy.
I sat in the most English of cafés
With your daughter,
Who followed me
When I ran away.
"I can see
The resemblance,"
Said the waitress
When she brought
Our steaming tea.
Like two cats
Trying to catch a mouse,
Your daughter and I smiled, buzzing
With light feelings
That exploded
When she left into glee.
That night, you refused to say a word
To either of us.
Is silence an axe
Raised above the head?

Day seven. My father
Once leaped off a moving train
Or perhaps it was slowing
To a stop,
To see the footprint
Of an ancient god
Embellished with vermillion
Powder
And marigolds
Every morning for a thousand years.
Against the backdrop
Of eternal time,
I pierce the space between
My host and I
With fakes.
The wealth and property
Of my host
Require constant surveillance.
Turning the corner,
Unsurveilled,
I simulate the movements
Of an ape.

On the eighth day, you
Try again.
In the boutique, you buy
Pretty bras.
I press the plush white towel
To my cheek.
This is titration:
A few moments to feel like
A complete human being.
When you ask the question
Again, I'm caught off guard
To such a degree
That I want to fall to my knees
And weep until you leave.
But this is your house
And there's no law
That requires
What you're offering me to last
Or outlast
The moment I crossed your threshold
To eat this heaving plate
Of meat.

The art of crisis
Is that you no longer
Think of home
As a place for social respite.
Instead, it's a ledge
Above a narrow canyon.
This is where you shit
And sleep, dreaming one night
Of jellyfish
In an aquarium
In Berlin, a factor
Of your European
Stay.
Beneath your clothes, you wear
A corset
Of bones, oil and
Cabbage leaves:
A sticky paste.
This causes shame
When it's time
To disrobe
In the facility.

They tossed the garnet necklace
My mother gave me
When I was ten,
A brilliant child who studied
The history of revolutions
In school.
Is a poet
An imperial dissident, or just
An outline
Of pale blue chalk?
What happens to the memory
Of other languages,
Carried in the body as poetry,
When everyone on the periphery,
The people who memorise
These poems
On their long journeys
To other lands, is gone.
My ancestral line
Was decimated,
For example,
One hot night.

How do you live when the link
Between creativity
And survival
Can't easily
Be discerned?
The answer to this question
Brought me here.
My fingerprints bloom
On the cream-colored
Card.
Can you
Delete it?
And with a click,
A sideways glance,
The name a lover murmured
At 3 a.m.
Is groomed.
I remember when I
Was a treasured pet.
With casual greed,
How I licked
That salty cream.

Blue nitrile gloves.
A drawer that's not pushed in.
The Victorian
Seriousness
Of the man
Posing for his
Photograph, upright
And unsmiling,
His moustache and satin shirt
Fit for tea with a King.
So many of my experiences
Were about waiting,
Noting the reserve,
Anxiety and palpable fear
In those guarded
Rooms.
Perhaps you know
What comes next.
Perhaps you don't.
Perhaps you have lived your life
Without error, fortitude,
Or end.

We've come to tell you
How much we love you,
How well you're doing,
Squawks the angel,
Dropping her cloak.
But all I could think of
Was the predator, the one
Who stops the flow of life
With a sweet gaze,
Then rises up
To get you.
How can you tell the difference
Between the smoke
Of the angel's cigarette
And the loving, clear eyes
Of whatever it is
That wants you
To go deeper,
So deep that peacocks and lions
Preen and flex
In abundance,
Carved by a steady hand.

A door opened in the side
Of sheer rock
And I stepped through it.
Images of an alternative life
Filled my psyche
Like wet owls.
I could not bear the facial expressions
Of the people
I was closest to, a source
Of embarrassment.
And so I left,
Never to return
Intact.
Or to a home
That was intact.
Yes, just like everyone else,
I had to deal
With the strong feelings
That moved through my body
Like sheets of rain
Embossed
With navy blue diadems.

How to wash a heart:
Remove it then pack it
In ice.
Remove it then paint it
In the course of one afternoon,
Like Edvard Munch,
An artist in transit
Between loves, colors, afternoons.
The taste of lemon rind
Mixes
With the Norway of dried blood,
A country
I visited once.
The linearity required of immigrants
Ebbs.
There's a cost
To that refusal.
A small voice pipes up
To ask me what I need
Before I go on,
But I have no time
For babies.

Silk, rubies, scripture
Written from right
To left.
A shirt made from raw cotton.
Earrings
Torn from the ears
In one gesture.
A Raleigh bicycle.
All the Arden Shakespeares.
The nurse's cape I wore to university.
A painting of four houses
On an English lane:
Pale blue and a buttery
Yellow.
Oh, everything.
Shoes.
Either we dumped it off
Or it was taken from us
In a great boiling wave
Of human gain.
There's no such thing
As skin.

The host's gleaming hair
Responds beautifully to the shampoo
She has set out for us
To share.
What's mine is yours,
She says with a sweet
Smile.
I don't want you taking her out
Without asking me
First, she continues,
Holding her daughter tight
Against her side.
I can smell your body
Odor.
I can smell your vagina.
Are you wearing your genitals
As a brooch?
I imagine this is what is meant
By the gift
Of a douche
And the yellow bottle
Of medicated powder.

I want to be split
Into two parts
Or a thousand pieces.
I want you to touch
My cervix.
I want my dress
Shredded
And my life
Too.
Then tenderly resumed
Or banished.
Whatever you want to do
To me do it.
To this end, I invited you
Back.
But at the door
To my bedroom,
The host appeared
In her jammies.
Listen.
We didn't agree
To this.

When what you perform
At the threshold
Is at odds
With what happens
When the front door is closed,
Then you are burning
The toast
And you are letting the butter
Fester.
Verbally, you state egalitarian
Ideals.
Financially, you hook
That brown baby
Up.
But in private, when it's snowing
Or when the sun
Is ruddy, a speculative
Blob,
You say no.
No to the wet towel
On the bannister.
I've had enough.

The host-guest chemistry
Is inclusive, complex, molecular,
Dainty.
Google it.
Does the host envelop
The guest or does the guest
Attract diminished forms
Of love, like the love
A parent has for a child
In September
And January, when the child
Is at its most
Vulnerable?
Are these questions enough
To violate
Your desire for art
That comes from a foreign
Place?
What are the limits
Of this welcome?
After all, I don't feel anything
For you.

On the first night, we danced
To Mbalax.
On the second night, I roasted
Cumin seeds
Then sprinkled them on yoghurt.
Without words,
Your daughter and I
Drank water
From the bowls on the windowsill,
A traditional form
Of consumption.
This shit's not manageable,
I wrote
On the fourth night,
Something you underlined
And questioned
When you found my Diary
And read from it
Aloud.
Was this the moment
I became
An alien form?

I dreamed my grandmother
Was lying face down
In a cave, immersed
In the lightly flowing water.
I dreamed my grandfather
Was riding a motorbike
Without a head.
I dreamed my father
Was pouring me a glass
Of white wine
In the kitchen
As we waited for the yoghurt
To cool.
I dreamed my mother
Was crocheting the sun
Into a dress of copper, blue and yellow
Yarn,
Smiling and nodding
Even as a man
Unknown to my family
Span my body
From a rusted hook.

I want to wake up
In the arms of the person
I love
And drink coffee with them
On a balcony
That opens up to a forest
Where the moss
Glows green
In the pouring rain.
We are both
Poets
Or one of us is.
It doesn't matter to me
What this person does
For a living
Or who they are
Inside gender's
Hall.
Light a candle, beloved,
And lay me down
On the forest floor.
Am I your queen?

There's a knock on the door.
There's a hand on my arm.
Your daughter is screaming.
My eyes are on fire.
There's a knock on my eye.
There's a hand on my fire.
There's a break in the scream.
The scream is mine.
My scream is at hand.
It knocks on the land.
The land gives way.
I suck
The hole.
The hole has a rim.
And in these last moments,
I clock the look
That passes between you.
You and the officer
From the Department
Of Repatriation.
And understand.
This is your revenge.

Note on the Title

A heart appears in the air next to the body or bunched up on a T-shirt in the snow, in the film with Beatrice Dalle on the sleigh. A heart appears in the air next to the body, for a few moments, exposing what's inside to view. In the stories my mother told me, the border was dressed with organs. The two things, cinema and war, converge emotionally as the instinct to write about this image: the heart displaced from its context, a cavity.

Rosalie Doubal, a curator of live events at ICA London, invited me to develop a performance as part of the Kathy Acker exhibit in 2019. With my sister, Rohini Kapil, I created an installation, performance, poetry reading or ritual called *How To Wash A Heart*. What became clear to me as I worked with the title was that the very thing that makes poetry so great – the intensity of an image or the way it repeats – is not so great when it comes to your actual life. The evening ended with a question: What receives the blood? No, we exited through a side door. To dump a bowl of red water – melted ice cubes – on the Mall.

On the night I arrived in London, I received an email from Ankur Kalra, an interventional cardiologist in Akron, Ohio, asking me to blurb his poems, works of heartbreak and passionate love inspired by the Bhagavad Gita! The wifi was spotty and so, though I couldn't download his manuscript, I asked him to tell me about his own work. What can you tell me about the immigrant heart? "Yes," he wrote back, "this is the area of my expertise. Of course, anxiety and shock have an effect." And: "There's a medical diagnosis attributed to it: broken heart syndrome or Takotsubo cardiomyopathy. Takotsubo is the Japanese term/word for octopus trap. The heart gets 'stunned' during acute emotional/psychological stress, and it affects the heart muscle and its pumping function. It loses a lot of its pumping function and assumes the shape of Takotsubo; just its base moves. It can be life-threatening, is more common in women, and does recover/regain the lost function in several weeks' time after the acute stressor fades away/is absorbed or processed."

When the night of the performance came, I read this email aloud then tore my book in half, drenching it in the good blood.

Good Blood: a performance ritual created by Lygia Pape in 2002, in which two people sit facing each other on chairs. Each one holds an ice cube made of red ink in their upturned palm. Whoever's ice cube melts first, that person is the good blood. The instructions don't ask for silence, but often, when I've shared this practice in faculty trainings or poetry seminars, the participants don't speak. I had an idea for the ICA event that was about the audience members, seated, ice cubes dripping on the floor, exchanging stories from the back of their own hearts. But in the end, this was too complex. I had to get it back down to the real floor. And lower the sun through the roof at midnight. It is always midnight in the art museum. As the audience entered, I gave them an ice cube each, made red with little drops. I thought I would say something, but in the end it was simply that, a way to welcome people into the space without using any words.

So, the title for this book came from these experiences, which took place a few hundred yards from Buckingham Palace. Would you like me to write a poem about it?! I can.

How to wash a heart:
Like this.
On a Wednesday evening in early
June
When the delicate blossoms
Turn white then crimson
Then green,

The dressing room
Of the ICA
Is pleasantly cool.
Honey on toast
Brings the hornets,
My mother said.
I'm not your bag of bones
To kick around anymore.
Instead, I pour the kettle
Of hot water
Over the red ice cubes
In a rehearsal
That surprises me
With its strong emotion
And plumes of steam.

In writing these new poems, I diverged – almost instantly –
from the memory of the performance. Instead, as soon as I sat
down to write, I heard an unexpected voice.

This is the voice of this book: an immigrant guest in the home
of their citizen host.

The speaker is an artist.

The red and the heart and the ice speak through them.

These poems are an attempt to work out that relationship
which, so rapidly, begins to go wrong. The only real thing I
want to say about what happens in this house – or between
these subjects – is that I saw something, read something, online,
scrolling through my news feed, about a couple in California
who had offered a room in their home to a person with a
precarious visa status. The couple, who were white, had adopted
a daughter from the Philippines a few years earlier, and I
was so struck by the facial expression of the mother in the
newspaper photograph, the taut muscles around her mouth

as she smiled. I also felt something I could not put words to when I read her ornate way of describing the hospitality that she was offering. That year, I had also been reflecting on my experience in university settings: an outward-facing generosity or inclusivity that had not, always, matched the lived experience of moving through corridors and faculty meetings of the "mostly white" spaces that a private, liberal arts college in the United States so often is. And how the discrepancy between the two is often felt and fleeting, rather than seen. I began to wonder, in other words, what it was really like in that house. This said, I have been unable to find the article again and wonder if I am conflating the story of the adoption and the story of the lodger here. Perhaps I misread the soft tissue contractions around the mouth of a woman in a photograph I saw only briefly, and once.

What else? In the US and the UK, as I wrote this book, anti-immigrant rhetoric amped up. Perhaps, by the time you are reading these words, it is worse.

Acknowledgments

The phrase "imperial dissident" comes from Priyamvada Gopal's *Insurgent Empire: Anticolonial Resistance and British Dissent*, which I read as I was writing these poems.

Sara Ahmed's evocation of the university as a zone of "conditional hospitality" in *On Being Included: Racism and Diversity in Institutional Life* has been profoundly proprioceptive for me, as I know it has for so many others.

I am also deeply indebted to Sayra Pinto, Robert Bal, Mg Roberts, Eunsong Kim, Lucas de Lima and Truong Tran for sharing their non-suppressed thought and experience with me, at the intersection of race, poetry and institutional experience. I was similarly grateful to contribute to a conference on race, coloniality and poetry studies in Spring 2019, curated by Tonya Foster and Dorothy Wang at CUNY Graduate Center. Some of the ideas in this book were worked out in that talk.

Thank you, Rosalie Doubal and ICA London, for your support and trust.

As I was writing the last eight poems of this book, I was returning from a literature festival in Moss, Norway. Above the Arctic Ocean, I watched *The Deposit*, a new Icelandic film derived from the novel of the same name by Auður Jónsdóttir. I was astonished to be watching something that so much resembled the heinous plot of my own book of poems.

I am deeply grateful to have been awarded the Judith E. Wilson fellowship in poetry, at the University of Cambridge, which has allowed me to complete this book and now to edit it.

I want to thank Sandeep Parmar for suggesting Pavilion Poetry and putting me in touch with Deryn Rees-Jones. Sandeep is also the person I get to think through Partition and its after-life with, a texture present in these poems.

Thank you, also, Sharon Anhorn, for letting me write all day on your sofa, when the voice of this book first arrived, and for making me chamomile tea with star anise as I wrote without stopping until dusk fell.

K. is Kate Zambreno.

The image of a grey ribbon (slack then taut) comes from a story that Ellen McLaughlin told during the AROHO retreat in Ghost Ranch, New Mexico. The reference is to her play, *Mercury's Footpath*, in which Mercury leads people to the Underworld, tying a grey ribbon to their wrists.

The outline of blue chalk derives from the memory of preparations for a mud sculpture, the reclining form of a female Buddha that Sharon Carlisle constructed in my garden a few years ago.

The story of Bumma was told to me by my mother, verbatim, in a moment of caring and being cared for that was indistinguishable from creative pleasure.